W9-CCJ-061

A LATE FRIENDSHIP

The Letters of
KARL BARTH AND
CARL ZUCKMAYER

Preface by
HINRICH STOEVESANDT

Translated by
GEOFFREY W. BROMILEY

WILLIAM B. EERDMANS PUBLISHING COMPANY
GRAND RAPIDS, MICHIGAN

Copyright © 1982 by Wm. B. Eerdmans Publishing Company
255 Jefferson Ave. S.E., Grand Rapids, Michigan 45903

All rights reserved
Printed in the United States of America
Translated from *Späte Freundschaft*, © 1977 by Theologischer Verlag
Zürich

Library of Congress Cataloging in Publication Data

Zuckmayer, Carl, 1896-1977.
A late friendship.

Translation of: Späte Freundschaft in Briefen.
Authors' names in reverse order in
original ed. 1977.
1. Zuckmayer, Carl, 1896-1977—Correspondence.
2. Barth, Karl, 1886-1968. 3. Authors, German—
20th century—Correspondence. 4. Theologians—
Switzerland—Correspondence. I. Barth, Karl,
1886-1968. II. Stoevesandt, Hinrich. III. Title.
PT2653.U33Z48313   1982   832'.912 [B] 82-12905
ISBN 0-8028-3574-0

CONTENTS

66733

PREFACE

It caused a small sensation among the friends of Karl Barth when, at the end of May and the beginning of June in 1968, in a duplicated letter of thanks to those who had sent their felicitations for his 82nd and last birthday, they read that: "Finally, in high old age a remarkable new friendship has been my lot, namely, with the poet Carl Zuckmayer, whom I visited last summer in Saas Fee just before I fell ill and with whom I have entered into a lively correspondence. He has just paid a fruitful visit to me (on the occasion of the Basel premier of *Des Teufels General*), and he looked fairly good between my rigid walls of books. What a man he is! He can be very serious and also very merry."

It was no less astonishing, one might assume, to a wider public to whom the two names meant something, when in January 1970, thirteen months after Karl Barth's death, Carl Zuckmayer published his "Story of a Late Friendship." The news spread like wildfire. It would not surprise me if a count would show that the issue of the Zurich newspaper in which the essay appeared was quickly sold out. I myself remember immediately ordering and giving away a dozen copies and receiving delighted echoes from every quarter.

But most surprised and happy of all—and every word they wrote about it bears witness to this—were the two friends themselves when they entered into this relation that they had never hoped for and found it developing at once into a highly intensive friendship. Nothing in the previous life of either, or the circles in which they had moved, pointed to such an encounter. They had known one another only at a distance and known each other's works only very partially. Nothing prepared either of them for the overwhelming discovery of a spiritual kinship that they both felt in spite of the differences of which they were still conscious.

In the period between their first acquaintance and the death of the elder of them, they were granted only two personal meetings. On both occasions the conversation cried out for continuation, for extension to other themes; and to the profit of those of us who come later a substitute was found for the missing personal contact in the "lively correspondence" which meant so much to Barth that he mentioned it in his circular letter. Quotations from Barth's share in this correspondence reached the public through Zuckmayer's essay and resulted in a widespread desire to know in context the source of the quotations.

So far as Barth's share was concerned, this wish was met in part when in 1975 the Theologischer Verlag Zürich published Barth's *Briefe 1961–1968* (edited by Jurgen Fangmeier and Hinrich Stoevesandt) as part of the complete edition of Barth's works, and included in this volume all Barth's letters to Zuckmayer apart from one whole letter and part of another, which were withheld at Zuckmayer's request. [Summaries of these letters may be found in the English translation of Barth's last letters, *Letters 1961–1968*, published by Wm. B. Eerdmans Co., Grand Rapids, 1981.]

But this simply increased the desire for the other portion, Zuckmayer's letters to Barth. Instigated by readers—Frau Susanna Niesel deserves special mention in this regard—the plan was conceived, after Zuckmayer's death, of publishing the correspondence in its totality. Frau Alice Zuckmayer, to whose willing cooperation I am most indebted, took up the project with immediate enthusiasm and granted permission to print all her late husband's letters to Barth without any omissions. Barth's ideas on some unexecuted literary projects of Zuckmayer, which the latter did not want published while he was still alive, may also be read in this new collection. With the agreement of his heirs some other minor abbreviations in the previous edition of Barth's letters have also been dropped. Two short sections have still been left unprinted out of consideration for third parties. One of Barth's letters that Zuckmayer quotes from in his essay—it helped to set up the first meeting—seems to have been lost.

The collection is augmented by a letter that Zuckmayer wrote after Barth's death to Eberhard Busch, who was Barth's assistant and was writing his biography. A reprint of Zuckmayer's essay concludes the book. How important the friendship was to Zuckmayer he showed in the last year of his life when he included this essay in his collection *Aufruf zum Leben. Porträts und Zeugnisse aus bewegten Zeiten* (Frankfurt am Main, 1976, pp. 299–306). The editor and publishers are indebted to the S. Fischer Verlag for kindly granting permission to republish this piece along with the poem "To Fathers," which Zuckmayer composed for Peter Härtling's collection *Die Väter. Berichte und Geschichten* (Frankfurt am Main, 1968, p. 40) and sent to Barth.

Finally, Frau Erika Heuberger, for many years Carl Zuckmayer's secretary—note, however, that hers was *not* "the sorting hand" that, according to the essay, almost blocked the acquaintance—merits special thanks for the fine cooperation she has given. Her share in the publication of this book is hardly less than my own.

Basel, May 1977   HINRICH STOEVESANDT

TRANSLATOR'S PREFACE

Apart from their evident human interest and the general insights they offer into the lives of a great theologian and a great author, these letters have the special value of containing statements that help to clarify Karl Barth's much debated attitude toward reason and nature. Regarding reason, he quotes with obvious satisfaction how, when a naive student wanted to know what reason meant for his theology, he gave the terse reply: "I use it" (p. 43). Regarding nature, when considering the suggestion of Zuckmayer in an early poem that one may worship God in the bark of a tree, he grants that God is in the bark, but as Creator, so that one may worship him there "only indirectly, inclusively, and mediately," since it is to God as the Reconciler who "truly acts and speaks in Jesus Christ" that "worship truly belongs" (p. 13). Again, discussing the view of Max Born (quoted by Zuckmayer) that science is responsible for our modern spiritual debacle, he makes a distinction between nature and natural science, gladly conceding that "nature does objectively offer a proof of God, though man overlooks or misunderstands it," but not venturing "to say the same about natural science, whether ancient or modern" (p. 42). Plainly, Barth's pointed rejection of natural theology was not intended, then, as a rejection of nature itself as either God's creation or even his self-declaration, but rather as a rejection of the actual attainment (by sinners) of a true knowledge of God apart from his saving self-revelation in Jesus Christ. Similarly, the criticism of reason was not a plea for irrationality, but a negation of the ability of sinners to find God unless their reason learn from Jesus Christ and enjoy enlightenment by the Holy Spirit. The importance of these remarks for a balanced assessment of Barth's theology hardly needs further comment.

Pasadena
Whitsuntide, 1982

GEOFFREY W. BROMILEY

A LATE FRIENDSHIP

Dear Herr Zuckmayer,

Someone has given me a copy of your book *Als wär's ein Stück von mir* and I read it at a sitting. And now I am forced to say how great and profound is the fellow-feeling with which I have accompanied what you have written there. First of all, I simply enjoyed your style. Then I derived pleasure from your descriptions of landscapes and people on both sides of the Atlantic, your sketches of individuals who were close and closest to you, your impressions and attitudes in the various historical situations, in the narrower or broader sense, into which you moved, through which you passed—always the same person—and from which you emerged unscathed but more mature and with a new zest for action. Your disposition and approach in all these bright or dark processes has been truly uplifting to me. And finally I also took pleasure in the fact that in the end (after being shamefully run down in Zurich) you have become a citizen of Saas-Fee and therefore a compatriot of mine. What I am saying should be an indication to you that I am very grateful and that from afar I take pleasure in your simple humanity.

From afar! You do not know me, and may perhaps just have heard my name occasionally and then forgotten it. You are ten years younger than I. We are thus members of the same age and generation. The time before the great fall is very clearly before my eyes. The two world wars and the interval between them made great inroads in my own life. But you and I live and have lived in very different spheres. Much more than you, I am a child of the nineteenth century; and the modern world of letters, the theater, the cinema and—how shall I put it—noble Bohemianism, has certainly affected me but never grasped or touched me closely. Thus many or most of those who

3

became a part of you mean little to me. And, to my shame, I must admit that all that I had previously read or seen of yours was *Des Teufels General*. I am an Evangelical theologian, a pastor in Geneva and the Aargau for twelve years, then a professor for fifteen years in Göttingen, Münster, and Bonn, where I became unacceptable because I would not take the oath of loyalty to Hitler in 1935, and from then until 1962 a professor here in Basel. I have written many stout and slim volumes of practical, historical, and above all—do not be alarmed!—dogmatic theology. I now live in quiet but busy retirement. I value the presence of loving women, good wine, and a constantly burning pipe. Nor are the beauties of Oberwallis unknown to me. I say all this so as to tell you something about who is writing and who it is that takes such pleasure in thinking about you.

With all good wishes and greetings,

Yours,
KARL BARTH

May I be permitted to send you two samples of my own writing? One of them, which has just been published, is part of my main output; the other, which came out in 1956, represents an important secondary interest.[1]

---

[1]Barth sent Zuckmayer his two books *Ad Limina Apostolorum* (Zurich, 1967; ET Richmond, 1968) and *Wolfgang Amadeus Mozart 1756/1956* (Zollikon, 1956). The former gives an account of Barth's visit to Rome in 1966 and his views on Roman Catholic theology.

Saas-Fee, July 10, 1967

Dear Professor Barth,

After a long absence—first on an Italian journey that led me to Rome, then in hospital to recover from a concussion resulting from a fall—I finally came back home at the end of June, and to my delighted surprise found your letter and the gift of your two books. I may tell you very sincerely that among the many letters that I have received since the publication of my memoirs none has given me more pleasure than yours. It is amazing to me that you who are at home in such a different field of thought should feel so affected by the story of my life. Did you really think that I would just have heard your name occasionally and then forgotten it? Since you are a man who writes or speaks only what he thinks, you must have truly thought this in some hardly believable modesty. It would be a scandal for a writer like myself not to know and respect you. For a long time your work and activity and position have been of particular significance to me so far as I have read about them or had experience of them. To be sure, I have not read your *Church Dogmatics* and I am theologically unsophisticated. But I am one of those for whom God is *not* dead and Christianity, when properly experienced and lived, is still the message of salvation. And you are one of those, of the few, who in our day will not allow Christians to pension themselves off and live on the legacy of those who have gone before. You are one of the few pillars who across the centuries hold up the freedom of the Christian, which is supremely an obligation, like a heavenly roof over our heads. For my generation, which has had to experience the way in which both confessions gave their blessing to weapons on both sides in two world wars, it was by no means easy to maintain faith. You have been a help to both of us, to both Roman Catholics and Evangelicals.

The two little books that you were kind enough to send me I have read with the interest that I previously gave (and still do) to detective stories, to use your own phrase.[1] The letter on mariology particularly enthralled me. For me, unaffected by historical or theological considerations, it has always been, I might say, a joyous and festive concept that the handmaiden of the Lord is now exalted to be the queen of heaven. In addition to the Holy Trinity I like to have a queen of heaven, even though this may be more of a pagan desire for deification than a Christian idea. It has been with me since childhood, however, and I cannot do without it.

As a former acolyte in Mainz, who knew the Latin service by heart, I have difficulty with the new liturgy, but I believe we have found a good combination in our congregation here as you did in a village in Oberwallis.[2] We still sing the Gloria, Sursum Corda, and Gratias agamus, as well as the Paternoster, in Latin, and thus preserve the universal aspect.

I found your work on Mozart, that little but infinitely rich symphony in four movements, surprisingly beautiful. And how right you are that this child prodigy never really was a child, and perhaps for this reason attained to the freedom of "great and free objectivity."

I thank you most sincerely for your letter and your writings. God be praised that in your advanced age he has granted you the joy of militant questioning, productive speech, and, after severe trials, love of life. May your glowing pipe not go out for a long time! I thus greet you with all good wishes and thoughts "from afar" in Oberwallis and from the closeness of a common citizenship that has become mine very late and after many wanderings,

With sincere respect,

Yours,
CARL ZUCKMAYER

[1] See *Ad Limina Apostolorum*, p. 63.
[2] *Ibid.*, p. 13.

July 12, 1967

This is my house in Saas-Fee[1]—some fifteen minutes outside the village, toward the north, and little affected by the stream of tourists who, especially in winter, use the ski lifts to the south.

I write under the gable or in the woods of larches and firs,

With sincere respect,

Yours,
CARL ZUCKMAYER

[1]Zuckmayer wrote this on a postcard with a view of his house; it was obviously a postscript to his letter of July 10.

Dear Herr Zuckmayer,

Since the beautiful 28th of July, when I visited your house with members of my family, you have heard nothing directly from me. That day was the highpoint of my stay (perhaps the last) in the Valais mountains. And the highpoint of that highpoint was undoubtedly the private conversation that I had with you. Rarely have I found a personal meeting so delightful as the unexpected one that I had with you. The good Rhine wine that you gave me as a parting present I have kept for some solemn festive occasion.

Thanks for everything, but especially for the works, previously unknown to me, among which the volume of stories has made the deepest impression. I do not really know to which of these varied but wonderfully harmonious pieces I should award the palm. All of them in their different ways have moved me deeply, and, if I know myself, and you as the author, they have done so—we spoke about this in Saas-Fee—in the thing which distinguishes you from Friedrich Dürrenmatt: in the never-failing compassion with which it is constantly given you to view human darkness, corruption, and misery. Mephistopheles is absent. In you the goodness of God which unobtrusively but unmistakably embraces all things and people governs and characterizes even the most trivial, bizarre, and foolish of scenes and situations. And the best is that you yourself hardly notice how much in what one might call your purely "secular" writings you have in fact discharged, and still discharge, a priestly office, and do so to a degree that is granted to few professional priests, preachers, and theologians, either Roman or Evangelical. I will not say anything about your poetic art, for I do not feel competent to do this. But as a layman in this field I may admit to you, without wishing to flatter you, that from the standpoint of your content I regard you as a poet of the first rank.

Since we came to speak about predestination in our discussion at Saas-Fee, I have since had my publishers send you one of the many volumes of my dogmatics in which I have dealt specifically with this subject.[1] I might well wonder whether you will be able to make anything of this specimen of academic Evangelical theology. If not, I shall not take it amiss. To make it easier, perhaps, I am having sent a little book of sermons preached in the prison here,[2] in which you will possibly see more clearly how I have tried to bring the same statement that is made in the big volume to the simple man, or not so simple in this case, and above all have tried to pray with this man.

. . . . .

Incidentally, my stay in Valais was interrupted by an unexpected new flare-up of my sickness in the lower regions, so that I had to travel by ambulance at night from the Val d'Hérens to the City Hospital in Basel and be given full medical treatment there. I am now back at home, rather the worse for wear, but on my feet, or rather at my desk. Hence my long silence.

I greet you as a friend, or rather as a younger brother, whom I found only late but with all the greater gratitude. Please pass on my greetings and thanks to your family, especially your wife. How lovingly and festively you welcomed our group that day in July,

With sincere affection,

Yours,
KARL BARTH

[1] K. Barth, *Die Kirchliche Dogmatik* II,2 (Zollikon, 1942), *Church Dogmatics* II,2 (Edinburgh, 1957).
[2] K. Barth, *Den Gefangenen Befreiung* (Zollikon, 1959), *Deliverance to the Captives* (London, 1961).

Sass-Fee, Sunday, August 20, 1967

Dear Herr Barth,

I have wanted to write you for a long time, for I must thank you for the gift of your book, whose arrival was for me a wonderful event. I did not know, however, whether you were back at home yet—I only learned through a telephone conversation between my daughter and your son that you had not been well. I was afraid the exertion of your trip to us might have been responsible. I am all the more happy to learn, therefore, that you are now back at your desk, I hope with a proportionate measure of health.

I do not know how to thank you for your letter and for sending the two books (*Dogmatics* II,2 and the sermons *Deliverance to the Captives*). All this and your affection, what I might almost call your fraternal and paternal friendship, is for me a true ray from heaven, a wholly unhoped for, unexpected, and unmerited grace, such as life seldom confers. I could never have dared to think or hope that my works, which were often written with a certain lightness, or at least lightheartedness, would be able to speak to someone like yourself. And you are quite right, I have hardly noticed, if it is true, that in my natural love for the world and its Creator (or the compassion that I regard as a self-evident emotion or task for the poet) there is enclosed a kind of priestly activity. "Mephistopheles is absent," you write. Others, especially professional critics, have often regarded this as a defect in my work. One dear lady friend, now deceased, once said to me that I never portrayed a wicked person with whom there could be no sympathy (rightly, I did not regard the vicious Nazi in *Des Teufels General* as a true person, but as a mere functionary or function of evil); and to do battle against evil by pinpointing it and denouncing it is the duty of authors precisely in our age. Portraying a supposedly holy world would

10

be a falsification, since there is no such thing. I replied at that time: "Who can prove that there is redemption? But we must and should hope for it, believe in it, and love it." I believe that the expression of goodness is a strong weapon in the fight against evil, whose depiction is not only not totally renounced but is even undertaken with a certain pleasure, and indeed a self-indulgence, by many authors. To know the wicked spirit but to summon up the good seems to me to be worth attempting. Your words, and the meeting with you, strengthen me in this view.

Now let me thank you particularly for the confidence you granted me in our (to me) valuable talk even though you hardly know me. I believe a person is visited and blessed by the good spirits of life so long as that person can love even in an "earthly sense." But perhaps it is not possible to fish for men[1] to whom one brings more tenderness than sternness. When sympathy persists, it is prayer.

Warmest greetings from my family and all good wishes for your health. As soon as possible I will arrange a trip to Basel so that I may visit you, and I hope that even if your health is none too stable you will still have the uninterrupted mental freshness and vitality that sparkles from your alert and strong eyes.

In grateful and sincere friendship,

> Yours from the heart,
> CARL ZUCKMAYER

I have just come from mass and am spending Sunday reading your sermons and prayers for those in prison. For the volume of the *Dogmatics* that deals with the problem of predestination, I will find some period of quiet; the weeks of summer are too busy for it, but I hope to be less occupied in the fall. Thanks again.

Please pass on our sincere greetings to your dear and honored wife, your son, and your pipe-smoking daughter-in-law.

[1]Luke 5:10.

Dear Friend Zuckmayer,

Last Sunday we heard, at least in part, your *Katharina Knie* on the radio. Were you yourself satisfied with the production? My second son, whom you do not know, and who in a month will move to Mainz as Old Testament professor, was also in the party, and he was no less interested in the dialect, which he and his wife, who is from Geneva, and his young children, who have had to learn Indonesian, then French, then Swiss German, will all have to get used to.

Your lively and moving *Katharina* spurred me on to answering your letter of August 20. We old life's warriors (who also enjoy life at times) do not want to let our encounter lapse so long as we journey on in the evening "accompanied only by the sinking star."[1]

Your plays have spoken to me with no less vividness—and with no less an impression of profoundest fellowship in the first and last and highest things—than your stories. I have had the greatest difficulty so far with your poems. But this is no doubt my own fault, because a direct but also exact and intimate relation to animals and plants, to earth and air and heaven, is not by a long way so natural to me as it is to you, as may be seen clearly enough in all your other works; or, more comprehensively, because the lyrical dimension, which is undoubtedly part of the fullness not only of poetry but of humanity in its fullness, is much more weakly developed in me than it is in you.

Resuming our first personal conversation, and perhaps preparing the ground for what I hope will be a continuation, may I ask you a question that troubles me a little? You suggested the possibility of worshiping God in the presence and even in the form of the bark of some Alpine tree. You know that Goethe once said something similar with reference to the sun.[2] From you, as distinct from theologians, I am willing and ready to accept such things and to take them in good part. Last time I wrote, I said that I view your literary work as a *priestly* ministry. And you clearly accepted this even if with some surprise. God is in the bark of a tree—I accept that. But the God in the bark of the tree is God the Creator (I have tried to understand and praise him as such in no less than four part-volumes of my *Dogmatics*[3] with which I will not burden either your bookshelves or yourself). In *priestly* ministry, however, we have to do with God the Reconciler of the creation that has fallen away from him and is indeed fighting against him. This God is certainly one and the same as God the Creator, but he is the God who truly acts and speaks only in Jesus Christ. It is to him and him alone that *worship* truly belongs, to him in his living Word as this is attested by holy scripture, or, for you Roman Catholics, to him specifically in his presence in the eucharistic offering—and to God in the tree-bark only indirectly and inclusively and mediately. Nor will you fail to see that whether the priestly ministry is discharged by an office-bearer or by what is called a layperson (I do not like this term or the whole distinction), even according to the statements of Vatican II it is an analogous participation in the priestly office of Jesus Christ which cannot be separated from his kingly and prophetic offices: implications in the light of which worshiping God in the bark of a tree seems to be very dubious even on the part of laypersons, even if these persons be poets like yourself, so that it should be mentioned only with the greatest circumspection and caution.

You will notice that in this excursus the theologian in me is showing his horns. He had to do this for the sake of honesty, and he asks pardon from the poet, but also understanding and reflection.

On another matter, you must have had some acquaintance with the dramatist Ginsberg, who died not so long ago after a severe illness; perhaps you knew him personally, since he must surely have crossed your path in Berlin twenty years ago. But so far as I remember—did I miss something?—he does not occur in the story of your life. He for his part mentions you in his book *Abschied*, edited by Elisabeth Brock-Sulzer, referring in not very complimentary fashion to a play that I do not know, and that he judges "not to be your strongest work."[4] He made a deep impression on me as a man (I was once with him in Zurich in 1945), in his love poems, and even more so in the poems written during his severe sickness. What did you and do you think of him?

Now another matter: What do you think of the double superlative that Goethe uses of his lost Ulrike when, thinking of her in the Marienbad Elegy, he calls her "the dearest of the dearest"? You will realize in what connection I am asking this.

My health has not been brilliant these last days, and there have been accompanying physical and mental fluctuations. My wife and my doctor and friend—who is also a Roman Catholic—are doing all that is possible and their very best to support me and cheer me up. I hope that you for your part have now recovered fully from the results of your accident.

In closing, may I ask you to do something for me, namely, to pass on my pressing thanks to your son-in-law, Herr Guttenbrunner, for the trouble he took to pass on the bottle of Rhine wine, which miraculously doubled itself in passing through his hands. My wife has already done this provisionally in a note to Frau G. But I ought particularly to thank Herr G. for the beautiful letter he wrote me on August 16. I hardly recognize myself in the closeup of my person and the spiritual light which he sees and depicts as radiating from me. But he meant it well, and I want to pass on friendly greetings to him and would be glad to see him again some day.

The members of my household join in greeting you. I never tire of recommending your books to my family and acquaintances in the narrower and wider sense.

Yours sincerely,
KARL BARTH

[1]From the last verse of Gottfried Keller's *Abendlied*.

[2]Goethe in his last conversation with Eckermann on March 11, 1832.

[3]*Kirchliche Dogmatik* III,1–4 (Zollikon, 1945–1951), *Church Dogmatics* III,1–4 (Edinburgh, 1958–1961).

[4]Ernst Ginsberg, *Abschied. Erinnerungen, Theateraufsätze, Gedichte*, ed. E. Brock-Sulzer (Zurich, 1965). Here (p. 148) Ginsberg says that shortly before Brecht left Zurich they were playing Zuckmayer's *Der Schelm von Bergen*, "not one of his best pieces," and after the dress rehearsal, when Zuckmayer asked Brecht how he liked it, the latter looked around the stage, found a helmet, put it on, lowered the visor, and said clearly and loudly behind the metal: "As an old warrior it pleases me fine." Which really said all there was to say.

Dear and honored Friend,

I am venturing to write this encouraged by your beautiful letter of September 12, for which I have long since wished to thank you. But I lost several weeks due to various matters both pleasurable and painful: the pleasurable, a couple of concerts in Lucerne and then the conferring of Pour le Mérite in the German embassy in Bern; the painful, dental treatment necessitated by a gathering in the upper jaw which more or less incapacitated me for almost three weeks. Your letter cheered me up during this period. The radio version of my old play *Katharina Knie* was done some years back. It was made enthralling for me by the voice of the actor Albert Bassermann who had performed in the opening in 1928; this rendering for Radio Basel was one of his last performances. He was one of the truest and noblest characters that ever trod the stage. I was to have paid tribute to him in Mannheim National Theater on the commemoration of his 100th birthday but was prevented from doing so by my dental problem.

I can understand very well that you find my poems more difficult than my plays and stories. They are not pure lyrics in which I was trying to develop this particular poetic form or to fill it with new content, but more occasional pieces, as Goethe called some—and not the worst—of his lyric poems. They sprang out of youthful feelings that often ran to excess. We are like theologians in this. Naturally you are quite right, and I agree wholeheartedly, that the admiration of God's power that may be evoked in observers by the bark or growth of an Alpine larch (this was the tree at issue) must never be equated with *worship*, not even by a poet. Like the luminous October days that we are now experiencing, it may awaken reverence and grateful devotion in us; that is, it may spur us, or even

16

force us, to prayer, raising love of the world to the love of God that expresses itself in prayer. But worship belongs only to him who, as you put it, truly acts and speaks only in Jesus Christ. Yes, in my youth I did incline to a kind of pantheistic animism, but at root this was only poetic exaggeration, an enhanced feeling for life—"feeling is everything"—and it has nothing to do with religion, except in "mood." Only later in the course of life's changes and chances and some serious thinking have I found my way back to the worship of God in his pure form as he manifests himself to us in the eucharistic offering. The bark of the larch is still a part of the beauty which lays hold of us on earth, and in which his love and grace manifest themselves—no more.

You ask about Ernst Ginsberg. I knew him well and thought highly of him, both as an artist and as a person. If, like many others worthy of mention, he does not figure in my memoirs, this is simply because he did not play any special role in my life. I had to cut down and tell only about particular milestones. I seldom saw Ginsberg after the time with Reinhardt in Berlin, and his maturity and severe illness came during a period outside the scope of my book. It is amusing that his anecdote about me and Brecht is without factual basis. I never saw the play *Schelm von Bergen* in Zurich, was not present at the dress rehearsal, and was also not intimate with Brecht. It may be that Brecht was present alone and made an ironical remark to someone else, but I was not there. Ginsberg, of course, believed I was; our memories often deceive us in this way—I have tried to guard against this so far as possible in my own memoirs.

As for Goethe's double superlative, I see only one interpretation, though I don't know whether it is valid. "The dearest of the dearest" is an imaginary figure that never really existed, almost a dreamlike apparition, of a perfection that is possible only in artistic constructs or visions, and that a real beloved, or dear one, cannot attain to when seen with the eyes of reality; Goethe has an imaginary picture of this dearest that is free from all the defects (even physical) that make us human, and he finds a certain happiness or consolation in putting her in the suprahuman or suprapossible sphere by using the double superlative. Is this an acceptable explanation? I do not know. But I think so.

Your article on the ban on Jesuits and monasteries in the *Basler Nationalzeitung*[1] has just come and it is marked by a high sense of justice (with your usual modesty you will say it is all self-evident)—but will it be heeded? The mills of justice grind slowly—though it must surely occur to any reasonable person that the age of *Pater Filuzius*[2] is long since past and there is no more danger to be feared from this quarter. There are other dangers on which I am at the moment reflecting a good deal, since I have to give a lecture to the students at Heidelberg in November.[3] But more of this some other time.

For today my very best and sincerest wishes for your health and well-being, and respectful compliments to your wife. My own family sends sincere greetings, and I will pass on your friendly greetings to Herr Guttenbrunner, who is at the moment in Vienna with his wife and child,

Ever yours,
CARL ZUCKMAYER

[1]K. Barth, "Jesuiten und Klöster," *National-Zeitung* (Basel), Oct. 7/8, 1967.

[2]*Pater Filuzius*, a satire on the Roman Catholic clergy, and especially the Jesuits, by Wilhelm Busch (1872).

[3]Zuckmayer's Heidelberg address of Nov. 23, 1967, "Scholar zwischen gestern und morgen," was published in *Neue Rundschau* (1968), pp. 1–15.

Dear Friend,

The fact that with great reverence and enjoyment a small group of us has just emptied the bottle that you sent is a reminder that I should answer your good and instructive letter of 10.9. There is something special about your Rhine white wines. Along with them I am always impressed by the French Haut-Sauternes, and earlier I was not a little fond of the rather sharp Neuenburg white wine. In this field I now particularly like the Valais Johannisberger and Fendant and some of the Waadtland wines, though they are not quite on the same level as the first two mentioned.

It was with sympathy and sorrow that I heard about the medical treatment you had to undergo. I hope that the worst is now behind you.

With some hesitation I congratulate you on your Pour le Mérite. Not that I remotely question your "merit," but the Bonn government that has conferred it is not one of the favorite objects of my admiration—it has not been since the age of Adenauer (with whom I once had an evening meal in Godesberg in 1946 and plunged at once into disagreement!), and it is not so now in its present form as a coalition, both on account of its foreign policy (its stubbornness toward the East and especially East Germany) and on account of its domestic policy (its emergency measures). In addition, a supposedly "Christian" party is in principle an abomination to me, especially when it is in power. But dubious people occasionally do something good. And they have certainly done so in conferring this honor on you. Perhaps you will show it to me if good angels should some day bring me to Saas-Fee. And perhaps in return, if you should manage to visit our humble abode, I will show you the gold chain that no government official but the rector of the University of Bonn hung around me on my 80th birthday to signify that I am "honorary senator." We are both people, are we not, who can have a good laugh at such things.

Last Saturday, being still active a little as a professor emeritus, I began a two-hour a week seminar, as I have done the last two semesters. This time we are studying the Vatican II constitution *On the Church*. In a salutary way this has made me put in a good deal of work, but it has also given me much pleasure, both on account of the material and also because I greatly enjoy dealing and speaking with the (some) 60 young people who are taking it, to whom I might well be a grandfather, but who with great kindness and respect let themselves be nourished by me, so long as I can still do it.

Did you experience any of the turmoil of the Confederate elections? The Valais Socialist Dellberg, who is my age and no longer endorsed by his own party, ran magnificently on his own and was convincingly reelected! Magnificent, too, was the election of cabaret star Rasser in Aargau Canton! But here in Basel a good and worthy man was rejected because he was "already" 71 years old. My wife and I spent hours at the radio to get news from the different cantons of our beloved country, interrupted only by American songs and military marches. Some day you must write a story in which you can describe and do honor to the old and young Swiss oddities whose fellow-citizen you now are.

It is to be feared that nothing decisive will come out of the bishops' conference newly concluded at Rome, at least not in the prickly matter of mixed marriages. From the very first I did not like the far too full agenda of this assembly. I hope that it is clear to you that in both thought and word you have much to contribute within the framework of the much-cited "lay apostolate" (I am constantly urging this on my doctor, too).

The poor pope, from what I read in the newspapers, suffers from much the same trouble as I do (prostate) and from the very same bacillus (it is called proteus mirabilis!) on account of which I have had to have two operations, and from which I still suffer (though the last weeks have been quite tolerable). Because he received me so graciously last year, I have told him this in a letter sent for his 70th birthday and wished him a new year of life filled with "wise resolves and courageous actions."[1]

My second son has now actually taken up residence in Mainz with all his family and started work there. They live on the Steig, obviously an eminence in that city, with which I am not acquainted. My other daughter-in-law, whom you know (the one with the pipe), has just wrecked her car, but along with three American passengers escaped with only slight injuries.

My own latest news is that I have been invited by Harvard University (Mass.) to give three lectures in December 1968. Can I do this, and can and should I accept? My wife and doctor would have to go with me.

Do you know the pretty little story about Pablo Casals? He is now 90 years old—so much older than either of us—and he still practices four to five hours every day. When asked why, he answered: "Because I have the impression I am making progress."

Please pass on greetings to your honored wife and tell her that *her* book, too, is read with great pleasure in our family.[2]

With all good wishes for spirit, soul, and body,

Yours,
KARL BARTH

[1]For Barth's letter to Paul VI, dated Oct. 3 1967, see *Briefe 1961–1968* (Zurich, 1975), pp. 432ff.; ET *Letters* (Grand Rapids, 1981), pp. 268f. (No. 267).

[2]Alice Herdan-Zuckmayer, *Die Farm in den grünen Bergen* (Hamburg, 1949).

Dear and Honored Friend,

I have been owing you a letter for a long time, but we only got back yesterday from a long and strenuous trip, and in the meantime I have had another attack of emphysema-bronchitis. For today, then, I will simply wish yourself and your dear wife and family a blessed Christmas and a happy New Year,

Yours most sincerely,
CARL ZUCKMAYER AND HIS WIFE, DAUGHTER, AND
SON-IN-LAW

A small, liquid greeting will follow by messenger next week!

Saas-Fee, February 19, 1968

Dear and Honored Friend,

To my distress I heard some time back that your dear wife has not been well—there was talk of a heart infarction, but I hope she is over the worst and is well on the way to recovery. I now hear from your daughter that you yourself had to go to hospital with a lung infection. But she also writes that you are both in relatively good shape, so I hope that this letter will find you steadily improving.

I find it most impressive and noble of you that in spite of your years and many problems of health you are holding your seminar on the council. But as long as you draw breath you will certainly not be able to live without doing something! Now at last I too, after losing a year on correspondence and necessary tasks of a more or less unproductive sort, am applying all my resources to a big new work about which I would like to tell you—but it is not far enough along yet; in the early stages there is always the danger that one can destroy something by talking or writing about it. "Its place is still within," I am told. But I think the material and the idea and, I hope, the eventual execution will meet with your approval.

It was with some hesitation and an understandable scepticism that you congratulated me on Pour le Mérite. I want to thank you for your felicitations, but should tell you that I did not receive this order from the Federal Republic, even though it was handed over by the chancellor of the order in the house of the very sympathetic ambassador, but from the chapter of members, which is made up of people of great integrity. This order (for arts and sciences, founded by that most intelligent of Prussian kings, Frederick William IV) dissolved itself in 1933—no Nazi ever received or wore its insignia—and it was revived by the renowned Theodor Heuss in the first year of his presidency of the Republic. One may thus accept the honor with every confidence. (Among its first recipients were Alexander von Humboldt and Jacob Grimm!)

We are planning to visit Basel in May for a new production of my *Des Teufels General*, and I most sincerely hope that you and your wife will both be well and we shall be able to visit you.

With warmest good wishes and greetings from my wife and myself,

Always yours,
CARL ZUCKMAYER

6 6733

Basel, March 16, 1968

Dear Friend,

Since November 1 you have heard nothing directly from me. If only you could guess to whom I have just sent a letter an hour ago! To no less a person than Pope Paul VI, who seems in some way well disposed to me, and whom I have now had to thank—at last—for various things.[1] You are next on the list immediately after His Holiness.

You have heard through my daughter what we have been through in these months and weeks that I hope are now not far from ending. I hope that she also expressed suitable thanks for your fine gift of wine. She is at the moment living with her husband not far from you in Grächen (above the village of St. Niklaus, which came to be of such significance to me, in the Zermatt valley). She toyed with the idea of visiting you in Saas-Fee, but in all friendliness I advised her that you are much sought after and very busy, and also that you and my son-in-law, a person whom I greatly admire in his way and who is truly very dear to me, would not hit it off too well.

Here we are now back to normal, at least in the sense that both my wife and I are out of hospital and thus moving about—if with muffled drums[2]—in our own place. My wife dare not risk a second heart attack. As for me, I can only be amazed that the good Lord deals with me with such goodness and patience and constantly surrounds me with such good people. When only a few days out of hospital, I found myself actively taking part in a kind of summit conference between Roman Catholic bishops and the corresponding dignitaries on our side.[3]

In literature, two people have claimed my attention these last weeks. The first, filling a long-standing gap in my education, is Wilhelm Raabe—his *Chronik der Sperlingsgasse, Apotheke zum Wilden Mann, Akten des Vo-*

Lincoln Christian College

gelsangs. The second is Jean-Paul Sartre, whose autobiography *Die Wörter* has been published in German by Rowohlt, along with his better-known works. Both have touched me, but in a rather *sinister* way. Raabe with the primitive German amiability of his depictions seems to me to be one of the most refined representatives of the secret nihilism of the nineteenth century, while Sartre with his hardly incidental ice-cold sharpness in relation to himself seems to be the crude representative of the open nihilism of the present century. Do you see either or both of them differently? You are really better qualified than I am, so during a pause in your work please tell me briefly what you think.

I was rather dumbfounded by one statement in your last letter, namely, when you called Frederick William IV the most intelligent of the Prussian kings. He did not seem to act very intelligently in the Berlin revolution of March 1848 (his younger brother, the later king and emperor William I, the "grapeshot prince," no more or even less so). From my own reading of history, Frederick William, indeed, was obviously mentally ill—at least in the last years of his life. And as a Swiss I obviously cannot approve of the fact that if he had had his way (the Prussian order of battle was already set up), there would have been war between Prussia and us in the fifties on account of Neuenburg; Napoleon III and the English intervened and averted this disaster.

Do you know what has happened to me—something almost on the same level as your elevation to the knightly order Pour le Mérite. I was hardly out of hospital before the solemn news reached me from Paris that I had been elected a member of l'Institut de France (Académie des sciences morales et politiques)—replacing a deceased brigadier general! I still had to learn that in France this was an honor in possession of which I could end my days, along with thirty-nine other rustics, only a few steps beneath Charles de Gaulle, and wearing a gold-flecked uniform and a dress-sword. This is something else we might have a good laugh about.

Please tell your honored wife that I have greatly enjoyed reading *her* book too, from A to Z.[4] In its own way, as is proper, it is worthy to stand alongside your own works.

This coming summer semester—if God wills and we live[5]—I plan to study Schleiermacher again with my students. Does the name of this man (born 1768) mean anything to you? I have fought my whole life long against his Romantic theology and at the end want to try to shed light on it for the young people of today. Can I do this?

And now we are looking forward to seeing you and your *Des Teufels General* in Basel in May. As regards arrangements here on the Bruderholz,[6] I must try to make plans depending on how many hours you can grant us. Many who are close to us will naturally want to get to know you personally. But again and above all I should like to make use of this occasion for a private talk. In any case, because of the uncertain state of our health you will have to be content with the most modest of receptions. Yet "one way or another," as the greatest general of all times[7] used to say or shout, you will not miss out on the Bruderholz, where we think of you with great affection.

Our best wishes and greetings to you and yours, including those in Vienna,

Yours,
KARL BARTH

[1]For Barth's letter to Paul VI, dated March 16, 1968, see *Briefe 1961–1968*, pp. 462–464; ET *Letters*, pp. 285f. (No. 281).

[2]An allusion to Adelbert von Chamisso's poem *Der Soldat*.

[3]At this conference (February 28, 1968), Barth gave an address on "Kirche in Erneuerung." Cf. Zuckmayer's letter of April 10, 1968.

[4]Alice Herdan-Zuckmayer, *Die Farm in den grünen Bergen*.

[5]James 4:15.

[6]The Bruderholz is the district in the south part of Basel where Barth lived.

[7]Adolf Hitler.

Dear and Honored Friend,

It is high time for me to answer your loving and rich letter of March 16 which—a great honor for me—you wrote immediately after writing Paul VI. What pleased me most was the news that you are both back at the Bruderholz, and, God willing, are on the way to recovery and better health. Your wife must take care and not burden or exert herself with visits of any kind. I believe that a heart infarction can heal up at her age but it needs much rest, unbroken sleep, and taking things easy, that is, not forcing oneself when tired. So I tell you ahead of time that we both beg you most urgently not to make our visit—for we will naturally come—the occasion of any kind of exertion, especially in the form of hospitality; we do not have to come to a meal and will adapt ourselves fully to yourselves and your manner of life and whatever you have in view, whether in the morning or afternoon or any other suitable time. I myself am not very anxious to make many new acquaintances. What I want most is a talk with you. But if there are people who are close to you to whom you would like to introduce me or both of us, please do as you desire. The opening of *Des Teufels General* in Basel is on May 16 and on this day the evening and the afternoon too had better be ruled out, for such occasions involve all kinds of demands when one is officially invited and, apart from the personnel at the theater, many people, known and unknown, lie in wait after the performance; and though such meetings are usually unprofitable and even in many cases very boring, one has to put up with them out of politeness. This is why for many years—unless it is an original production in whose preparation one plays an active part—I have avoided accepting invitations to such openings in any city, and I can tell you honestly that I have accepted in this instance only because you (and the zoo) are to be found in Basel. For I can see the Bernoullis[1] here as well; they come to their Almagell house every year. I shall keep May 15 and May 17 free for you to fix the day and time that suit you best. We shall arrive on the evening of the 14th and have to leave for Zurich on the 18th.

I have not read Wilhelm Raabe for many decades. I know the works you mention from my youth and will study him again, for there is in him a poetic version of the Pied Piper of Hamelin, a theme that has aroused my dramatic interest for some time,[2] not because someone blows a magic flute, but because of the youthful unrest and the exodus of the children, which is historically quite close to the children's crusades. I detect a kind of parallel to such modern phenomena as the curious wanderings of the so-called "hippies" in America, which undoubtedly do not represent only the usual social rebellion but include a kind of chiliastic trait. But first a much more serious and dramatic theme engages me—if only the good Lord will grant me the blessing of letting some gleam of light and cheerfulness shine on it. What I have in mind is a *Dialogue of the Condemned* from the resistance movement against Hitler. The idea is very different from that of *Des Teufels General*. It is not meant to be a character tragedy; I want to state clearly once again the political, intellectual, and religious testament of these people, which is partly talked out and partly forgotten—and to do so precisely at this critical juncture. Perhaps I may talk to you about some of them. You probably knew Dietrich Bonhoeffer and perhaps also Delp and others. I am not aiming to give portraits, but to capture the spirit. Please regard this as a very confidential communication. Apart from my wife and Gräfin Freya von Moltke, no one knows what I am working on, and for heaven's sake it must not become public or be an object of publicity before it has succeeded—or failed. It is as yet only an attempt—but I believe it is worth trying.

As for Wilhelm Raabe, apart from the grace of his narrative expression, I have felt in him a certain "craftiness"—

this is what my long deceased friend Heinz Hilpert, a Raabe expert, called it. Perhaps it is the same thing as what you feel to be secret nihilism. Sartre's work I have so far only in the French *Les Mots*, and in trying to read it I have noticed that my vocabulary is not adequate, so I will get the Rowohlt German edition. I can make no evaluation of this book, but his work in general (some of it fine drama) always leaves me with the impression of an ice-cold dissecting knife with which one peels an onion until finally there is no core left but only nihil.

How fitting are the words of Paul quoted in your work *Erneuerung der Kirche*,[3] for which I thank you and which I have read with excitement—including that about art, and especially drama, with *agathon* and *teleion* as content, and *euareston*[4] as form. In the best and most beautiful instances, as in your beatified (or to be beatified) Mozart,[5] there is complete fusion.

Bondage to the spirits of the age and to fads may be seen in a truly repulsive way today in literature, especially German literature. There is in it no trace of the "cheerful confidence"[6] which, one might have hoped, would have shone over us after the terrors of Hitlerism were overcome. But naturally one cannot have this without religion, which most of these people hardly take into account. I have just read a work, a kind of life-sketch, by the very respected physicist Max Born[7] (b. 1882), which ends in complete pessimism. He believes that the dominance of the natural sciences, which he himself has served and loved his whole life, is to be blamed for "the end of man as an ethical, free, and responsible being."

Perhaps I am naive, but all that I have learned through the natural sciences seems to me to be a kind of proof of God—metamorphosis, for example. Is Teilhard de Chardin too "monistic" for you?[8] His "créer, c'est unir," his grandiose attempt to portray the unity of spirit and matter, which is first and last complete only in God, has made a great impression on me. As I write this, I am looking out of the window, and two days before full moon (we have

Maundy Thursday in between) the moon is just coming up over the mountains in a clear sky. I am always gripped by a scene such as this; it bears testimony for me to the constant movement of the world, like the "pilgrim people of God," in the sphere of creation.

As regards *Erneuerung*, there is much to report here. I told you last summer that here in Valais we had worked out what I found to be a very fine "mixed" liturgy in which some parts of the mass were still sung in old style in Latin. But all that has now gone. Everything is in German. I think this represents to some extent an impoverishment. It is not true that people did not know the meaning when the Gloria, Credo, Sursum Corda, and Paternoster were sung in Latin. Many of the liturgical forms (I do not know whether they were Gregorian or post-Gregorian; they were certainly not pre-Gregorian) had a wonderful solemnity (including the Ite) or a profoundly oratorical impressiveness, especially the Paternoster. Now this is sung responsively by the priest and choir and almost in a monotone. How impressive was the *et ne nos inducas in tentationem*. The German translations also seem to me to be flat and colorless: *et divina institutione formati, audemus dicere* becomes "und angeleitet durch göttliche Belehrung wagen wir zu sprechen." Is this just the recollection of the Mainz acolyte who feels somewhat disillusioned? I am not what modern Roman Catholic clerics call a "religious Romantic." I would be happy if the Germanizing, or elucidating, or the general hearing of the sacred mass in the various national tongues would lead to a more genuine and intensive participation of the congregations, and especially of the young people. But I have some slight doubts whether this will come about. On Palm Sunday we were told for the first time that there is a new order that from this Easter, while the Lord's Prayer in the mass will still end with "deliver us from evil," as a prayer it should now include the ending "for thine is the kingdom," which so far has been customary only in the Evangelical church. In the "Hail Mary," too, the word "Frauen" is to be used instead of "Weibern" in "blessed among women." Is *in mulieribus* the same as *in feminis*? And why the weaker German word?

Well, I can only welcome anything that promotes unity or renewal. And I will relegate it to the sphere of "aesthetic reservations" if I miss hearing *flectamus genua* on Good Friday.

With Schleiermacher I have only a literary acquaintance, especially through his relation to the Romantics, the Schlegel brothers, and others; I recall his *Vertraute Briefe über die Lucinde*, and dimly his *Reden über Religion an ihre gebildeten Verächter*,[9] but theologically I have no knowledge of him at all, and in general only very little. I hope that you will publish what you have to say about him; it will help me to fill one of the gaps in my education (one of many).

I was guilty of a slip in my last letter; I should not have said that that Prussian king was the "most intelligent," but the "most cultured," as Alexander von Humboldt called him. Perhaps he was right, for Frederick the Great was very one-sided in his education.

I had just reached this point in my letter when my wife came and told me that she had heard on the radio that the German rebel Rudolf Dutschke had been fatally shot—by whom, it was not known, but thanks be to God, not by the Berlin police; apparently by some other youth. The news sickened me. Dear God, what times we live in— once again, or again and again, for ever? For ever? "But the sphere of God's creation is also the sphere of sin and death," I read in Karl Barth.[10] The hectic sociological jargon of Dutschke had little meaning for me, and even less his use of the term "revolution," which seemed in him to be without any real goal, only the destruction of the existing order in order that something new might emerge. Nonsense. We were already beyond that in the trenches in Flanders in 1917/18. But there was something serious about him. When I was in Germany last year I thought to myself that either we would have forgotten about him in two years or he would mature. Now he has been made a martyr—for what?

And this hardly a week after the assassination of Luther King. And in an obscure situation in international politics in which one can no longer distinguish with the naked eye between good and evil, or *agathon* and *teleion*.

By chance we then heard on the radio the wonderful black singer Leontine Price singing spirituals with a choir— "Come on, sweet Chariot" [sic]—this offered a kind of comfort. But if I tell one of my literary colleagues that for me the eucharist is real comfort—I was present last Sunday and will be again this coming Sunday—they regard me as crazy—a "babbling cannibal tearing his God apart" is what I read in one of them recently.

This is how one is jolted between the solemn march of the moon in the pale sky and the sparkling procession of the planets and fixed stars in the dark sky. It is now very quiet, and I know there is only one thing to do: give thanks to God.

I will send this letter off by express mail tomorrow so that it may reach you as an Easter greeting. I wish you both a joyous and healthy resurrection day,

Yours sincerely,
CARL ZUCKMAYER

P.S. Even though you think your son-in-law and I would not hit it off, I would have been glad to see them both, but we were away at the time. In the summer there is a magnificent mountain trail from Grächen to Saas-Fee, taking seven hours and going over 3000 m.; I did it two years ago and hope I can do it again.

[1]Basel friends of Zuckmayer.

[2]Zuckmayer's play *Der Rattenfänger. Eine Fabel* was finished in 1974 and received its first performance in Zurich in 1975, when it was also published.

[3]Barth had sent his address "Kirche in Erneuerung" to Zuckmayer as printed in the *Schweizer Rundschau* No. 3, 1968. The quotations from Paul may be found in 1 Cor. 6:12 and Rom. 12:2.

[4]Paul's terms are translated by Barth "the good," "that which leads to the goal," and "the fitting or pleasing."

[5]In the address previously mentioned Barth said: "I have no chance of being pope, but if I were I would beatify—not sanctify—this man Mozart, who was also a good Catholic."

[6]The phrases "bondage to the spirit of the age and to fads" and "cheerful confidence" are taken from Barth's address.

[7]Max Born, "Gedanken und Erinnerungen eines Physikers," *Universitas* 23 (1968), pp. 249–276.

[8]In his lecture Barth had criticized Pierre Teilhard de Chardin. Referring to the constant renewal of God's pilgrim people until we have "the absolutely new church on a new earth under a new heaven," he asked that we do not follow Chardin in speaking of a "point omega, which is supremely and finally to be found within the history of the world and the church."

[9]The reference is to two of Schleiermacher's earlier works, *Vertraute Briefe über Friedrich Schlegels Lucinde* (1800) and *Über die Religion, Reden an die Gebildeten unter ihren Verächtern* (1799); ET *Speeches on Religion* (New York, 1958).

[10]In the address "Kirche in Erneuerung."

Saas-Fee, Good Friday evening, April 12, 1968

Dear Friend,

By way of supplement to my letter of yesterday, which had a sad ring, I should like to send you something today that will cheer you up—I hope you will find it amusing. Some weeks ago I was pressured by a publishing house to write something for an anthology on "Fathers," in which grandfathers as well as sons were asked to take part so as to give a picture of the father, or the image of the father, in modern life, whether from a personal or a more general standpoint. I was afraid that a good deal of twaddle would be talked about the lost or outmoded image of the father, overworking that dreadful word "das image," a mangling of *imago* adopted from the American. Since I have said in my memoirs all that I can say about my father—for me a model I have always loved and respected—and have no desire to repeat myself or to take part in theoretical discourses, while on a walk I composed in five minutes a few verses which put me in a very merry mood.[1] We should not tackle even problems of this kind without humor. I ought to say that the Hessian-style rhyming of *Kindern* and *Hintern* had behind it the authority of Goethe, in whom there are hundreds of similar rhymes (for example: "Ach neige/Du Schmerzenreiche." Goethe, of course, pronounced neige "neiche," as everyone does between the Rhine and Main, Neckar, Nahe, and Mosel).

Again with fond Easter greetings,

Yours,
Carl Zuckmayer

---

[1]This poem first appeared in P. Härtling, ed., *Die Väter. Berichte und Geschichten* (Frankfurt, 1968), p. 40.

Den Vätern ins Stammbuch

Habt keine Angst vor den Kindern!
Sie sind nicht erhab'ner als Ihr.
Drescht Eurem Sohne den Hintern,
Eh' dass er die Achtung verlier'.

Kriecht nicht vor ihnen wie Sklaven,
Auch wenn sie meckern und schrein.
Selbst bei den kritischsten Schafen
Muss noch ein Leithammel sein.

Seid Ihr verkalkt und verblödet,
Fühlt Euch zumindest als Mist,
Denkt: jeder Acker verödet,
So er nicht vorgedüngt ist.

Wenn Ihr Fehler gemacht habt—
Wer war sein Leben lang klug?
Doch wenn Ihr einmal gelacht habt
Über Euch selbst!—ist's genug.

To Fathers for the Family Album

There's no need your children to fear!
For they are no better than you.
But paddle them well on the rear,
They'll give you the respect that's due.

Do not cower like slaves or creep,
For though they may grumble and plead,
Even the most critical sheep
Still need a bell wether to lead.

You may feel outdated and old,
And little more use than manure,
But dung is more precious than gold
If the crops are going to mature.

At times you may well make mistakes
For no one is right all the day
But a laugh is all that it takes—
To laugh at oneself is the way.

C. Z.

Saas-Fee, April 13, 1968

Mon Dieu,

With all the things I had to write about, I completely forgot to congratulate you on the great honor that was done you with your nomination as a member of the Académie of the Institut de France. I believe this is a very *unusual* distinction, especially for those who are not French, and I am truly delighted at it.

Penitently for my tardiness, but all the more sincerely,

Yours,
CARL ZUCKMAYER

Rome, April 22, 1968

Dear Friend,

We are here, God be thanked, only as "laymen," with nothing to do but enjoy the Roman spring and the wine of the country. Yet there is always a "mission": in a simple restaurant I suddenly came on an "ecumenical group" from Germany which knew me, and I had to speak to them!

Sincere greetings,
Yours,
CARL and ALICE Z.

Saas-Fee, May 3, 1968

Dear Friend,

I have reserved two seats for you for the opening of *Des Teufels General* on May 17, though this does not mean you have to be there.

I shall understand only too well if a fairly long evening at the theater is too much for you and your wife.

I would be grateful for a brief word whether you want to use the tickets or not. You can naturally pass them on to your son or daughter.

If not, I can dispose of them elsewhere,

With sincere greetings,

Yours,
CARL ZUCKMAYER

Dear Friend,

I have before me—since I last wrote—no less than four communications from you—each delightful in its own way. The time has now come—before your personal visit to our knee of the Rhine—to answer them. That it has only just come is due in part to crises in health which overtook my wife and to a lesser extent myself (we are doing better just now), and in part to the fact that these last weeks have been like old times, as I have been working so hard on my little bit of academic activity. It has been a real blessing that—almost directly from heaven—we have found an excellent and kindly disposed 62-year-old housekeeper, nurse, and very good cook. At 17 she was definitively frightened away from the Roman Catholic church by an indecent question put to her at penance, and since then has lived in an ecclesiastical vacuum, and for the first time is frequently hearing from us again about Christian things. She is called Frau Stöckli (sic), and will open the door and do the honors to you in the happy day of your visit to the Bruderholz.

To her real regret, my wife must excuse herself in advance for that day; on May 12 she has to begin a period of convalescence at Adelboden in the Bernese Oberland. As a grateful reader of your books, she will take along, among others, your wife's book (and I hope your wife will not fail to accompany you here).

Well then, the fifteenth or seventeenth of May! Naturally, accompanied by some kindred spirit, I shall be at *Des Teufels General* on the 16th. How, then, if you could spare an hour—an evening hour—on the 17th *after* we see and hear the play, and to allow you time for the zoo? And I will invite perhaps up to three select guests. But my own main desire is for a talk with you, and far be it from me

41

to make too many demands. Hospitality, then, in the form of light refreshment! Rather inadequate compared to a connoisseur like yourself, I am in a bit of a fix in this regard. But Frau Stöckli will help me. Your kind offer of two free tickets has just come. The kindred spirit who will come with me to the theater is my son Markus, who is known to you and whom I will put in the picture at once by phone.

Your inspired song to fathers pleases me greatly—though I have some doubts whether it is the right time for it. If there were a university with modern students in Saas-Fee, they might perhaps learn something! As a nonpoetic counterpart I am sending you seven rules of life[1] which I penned some two years ago (for myself) but which have now reached a wider public, as you will see. You might also find pp. 38ff. and 42ff. of the paper worth reading.

I knew Dietrich Bonhoeffer well. What he would have thought and planned and achieved had he lived, no one can say. The fragments of his theology (especially from his final years) have unfortunately become the fashion. To know him properly, the standard book is the great biography by Eberhard Bethge (Christian Kaiser Verlag, Munich). I would not say with Max Born that natural science is responsible for the modern intellectual and spiritual debacle. On the contrary, I would gladly concede that *nature* does objectively offer a proof of God, though man overlooks or misunderstands it. Yet I would not venture to say the same of natural *science*, whether ancient or modern.

I can understand your aesthetic problems with the postconciliar Catholic liturgy. The example you give ("angeleitet durch göttliche Belehrung") is indeed poor. But is it not true that the shaping of the liturgy is first and last a problem of church and theology? Could it and should it be expected in the long run that Christians in Ghana or Korea or even Basel and Valais should be edified in Latin? And how glad I am I do not have to pray the rosary, for I should find it hard to say "among women" in view of the present-day associations of this expression ("women become hyenas," "beware of women," etc.).

Schleiermacher: When you come I will show you two of my books in which I tried to expound him to the best of my ability.[2] If you like them I will have them sent on to you with pleasure. I am dealing with him in a seminar with many boy and girl students and for the moment I am enjoying it (with the old love/hate and the even older hate/love).

Thanks that you took the trouble to write a special letter about the Institut de France. My sense of things has not been altered in the slightest by this honor. And my bowel and bladder, those lowly brethren, have taken not the least notice in their conversations with one another.

. . . . .

I have all kinds of things to report. For instance, a very orthodox group of Roman Catholic vicars invited me for the second time to a lively hour-long conference. Again, we had a visit from a crazy woman from St. Gall who thought she was the woman of Rev. 12 and a reincarnation of Mary. Again, an immature theological student from Canada came to see me this morning and asked—among other things—what reason means for my theology. Answer: I use it!

Do you know the astonishing book about the excavations at Masada,[3] the desert fortress on the Dead Sea where in A.D. 73 (three years after the fall of Jerusalem) 930 Jews, at the end of their fight against the Romans, killed themselves and their wives and children so as to rob their victors of their triumph at least in this way? What strange things come to pass on earth, and can and will still do so! Plenty of material for stories and plays, dear poet-friend!

Well, we will soon see each other and have a talk. But I wanted to write something so that we would have subjects immediately to hand. When you come, however, I want especially to listen to you.

In great anticipation and with all greetings and good wishes,

Yours,
KARL BARTH

[1]Barth sent Zuckmayer a copy of his Rules as they were printed in the *Evangelical Digest* 10, No. 5 (May, 1968), p. 23. The other two articles to which he draws attention are W. Hammer's "Die Kirche stirbt nicht" and O. Gulbransson's "Gedanken zum Kirchenbau."

[2]Cf. *Die Theologie und die Kirche* (Munich, 1928; ET New York, 1962), pp. 136–199 and *Die protestantische Theologie im 19.Jahrhundert* (Zollikon, 1947) § 11 (ET Valley Forge, 1973), pp. 425–473.

[3]Yigael Yadin, *Masada. Der letzte Kampf um die Festung des Herodes* (Hamburg, 1967).

RULES FOR OLDER PEOPLE
IN RELATION TO YOUNGER

1. Realize that younger people of both sexes, whether relatives or close in other ways, have a right to go their own ways according to their own (and not your) principles, ideas, and desires, to gain their own experiences, and to find happiness in their own (and not your) fashion.

2. Do not force upon them, then, your own example or wisdom or inclinations or favors.

3. Do not bind them in any way to yourself or put them under any obligation.

4. Do not be surprised or annoyed or upset if you necessarily find that they have no time, or little time, for you, that no matter how well-intentioned you may be toward them, or sure of your cause, you sometimes inconvenience and bore them, and they casually ignore you and your counsel.

5. When they act in this way, remember penitently that in your own youth you, too, perhaps (or probably) acted in the same way toward the older authorities of the time.

6. Be grateful for every proof of genuine notice and serious confidence they show you, but do not expect or demand such proofs.

7. Never in any circumstances give them up, but even as you let them go their own way, go with them in a relaxed and cheerful manner, trusting that God will do what is best for them, and always supporting and praying for them.

Dear Friend,

Before I come to the Bruderholz, I want to send you the enclosed copy of a letter to Dean Geiger[1] to show how things stand there. You will be disappointed but will kindly understand that there are times when one cannot "preach" or even discuss. The discussion I conduct with myself in my work and my daily life is much too obscure and contradictory—even though a beautiful shore is in sight, I am still swimming and not yet on solid ground. And I thank God that he has thrust me out once again into stormy waters. I do not decline this discussion out of complacency, but out of conscientiousness. I can talk about this to you. Those who swim have to hold their breath until they reach the bank, or at least grasp a solid raft.

That I shall not meet your wife is something I regret, but the main thing is that she should get really well, and how good it is that you have found an excellent and worthy housekeeper! Unfortunately my wife, too, cannot come because she has had a return of a bad neck and tonsil infection—something she has suffered from for some time. The doctor demanded a week of bed-rest and treatment such as would not be possible on a journey. Fortunately, we have an excellent Valais girl, so that she is well looked after and can be at peace during the days of my absence. My own brother body often causes me trouble, but only on the margin, through problems of circulation, blood pressure, and the like—and from Basel I have to go to Zurich for a urological examination, though not because of any particular difficulties; I have had to have an annual check since three years ago I had a multilateral cyst taken from the kidneys, and my poor bladder is also showing signs of aging. You know what I mean from your own body in the worst possible way; for me these are only little things which I can live with quite cheerfully and which hardly disturb my work.

I will call you early (but not *too* early) on Wednesday, and we can decide when I should come. And I beg you and your housekeeper not to be worried about refreshments. I am not a notorious "gourmet" or "gourmand"; we need to keep that for feasts and festive occasions, not everyday life—and it is only rarely that I drink the great wines of my homeland, including the French. Usually I drink light wines which one need not sip but can drink without counting the glasses.

Your rules for the dealings of older people with younger are very sound, and I go along with them. What I had in mind in my little verses was really the treatment of children. If one has lived in America and seen in countless cases what *injustice* is done to children, one has enough of it. One sees too much that someone, hidden behind misunderstood psychoanalytical maxims, allows them to become little tyrants and ill-humored despots, despots whom adults crawl in front of for pure convenience, only to get peace; and one sees how this takes effect in the unfortunate adolescents when they, brought up without authority, are confronted with the difficulties of life. And it is just that which we experience here, as we adopt all that is negatively "American," even in speech (also in advertising, in reporting, and in the nauseating illustrated magazines), instead of the sincere humaneness and good will with which—believe it or not—most Americans are inspired. It is terrible how the ideas of peoples and nations can disintegrate and be distorted through power politics and uncontrolled propaganda. But all of us can only try to mind our own business.

I unreservedly agree that the liturgy must be a theological and not an aesthetic matter. And I was thinking more of the universality of the Latin mass than its beauty. But perhaps an ancient language can no longer discharge a universal task in a pluralistic world. At any rate, on Easter Day (we only went to Rome on Thursday) a visiting

47

father suddenly took the office in Latin again, apart from the gospel and some prayers, and celebrated in the traditional way, and our choir pealed forth the Kyrie and Deo Gratias with palpable joy. Afterwards I heard many of the local people, who are by no means "aesthetes," say what a fine mass we had had again. But perhaps they were the old, older, or middle-aged members of the congregation. The young people quickly adapt to German (and would do so even more if it were our original Valais dialect, which others would not understand). The main thing is that they still come. We have here a group of young men (the young women don't dare) who ostentatiously stay outside, with their hats on their heads, and smoke cigarettes until the office is over. They are not socialists but progressives (meaning that they are out for money).

How would it be if we came on Wednesday later in the afternoon and spent the evening—if that is all right with you? The theater tickets are on the way. I only hope that the long session will not be too tiring for you.

With all good wishes and greetings to your family—for now,

Yours,
CARL ZUCKMAYER

I am not sure about the evening of the 17th, as I have already been invited by other good friends to visit them on this evening and do not know whether I can refuse.

I don't know what the performance will be like on the 16th, and I have no control over it. One can have this only when present at the beginning of rehearsals.

---

[1]In his letter to Prof. Max Geiger, Zuckmayer refuses an invitation to address the theological students at Basel; the reason is the same as that given to Barth.

Dear Friend and Church Father of the Bruderholz,

Our stay in Zurich dragged on longer than expected, and I could not write there or else I would have thanked you long ago in writing for the beautiful and harmonious evening I spent with you. When we arrived back here just in time for Pentecost, I found your circular letter to friends who sent congratulations on your 82nd birthday, and I am doubly grateful again for the kind and truly friendly words with which you refer to me in it.[1] You almost make me "red with shame," as we say in Hesse—for I do not recognize myself by a long way and have real doubts whether I am the true human I should be, or if am trying hard enough to be so. It is certainly an encouragement and a new spur that you find in me serious and bright possibilities in this direction.

Had I known it would be your birthday on May 10 some Rhine wine would not have been lacking among your presents. I have noted the date for your 83rd birthday and, I hope, others. The evening with you, which I hope was not too long, was the highpoint of my Basel visit, though I met other dear and clever people, for example, Doris von der Mühll, Carl Jacob Burckhardt's sister. But I was very much at home in your study. I find that a place is never more comfortable than when bookshelves line the walls (I found the finely bound edition of your *Dogmatics* particularly impressive), and when it is impregnated with the atmosphere of quiet work and objectified by the drift of tobacco smoke. I picture the study of Jacob Grimm in much the same way except that it must have been rather bigger, for in the memoir by his nephew we are told that he used to pace up and down in it with large strides. We did not get on to the subject of Schleiermacher but I hope you will write up your seminars on him. It was a great pleasure for

me to see your home on the Bruderholz and the little garden[2] and the friends you invited, the excellent Dr. Briellmann and the charming Busch couple—in my younger
days I would have said the wife was a sight for sore eyes.
Nor will I forget Frau Stöckli, and I am glad you and your
wife are being looked after so well. Thanks again for those
hours. I slept that night with a feeling of enrichment.

I have to say that the opposite was true of the evening
at the theater. The performance and the play had an am-
bivalent and troublesome effect on me, nor could I take
much pleasure in the public acclaim. Naturally, as an author, when attending, one has to put on a good face at a
dubious show and not spoil the fun of the people at the
theater, who mean well. But a year ago I saw a performance
of the *General* at Berlin—one of the last appearances of
my friend Hilpert, who died in December '67; and avoiding
any bluster, and some real effects in the first act, he brought
out at once the true seriousness and tragedy, seating the
skeleton at the table, as was supposedly the case with Pla-
tonic guests. In this form the play had a strong impact on
the young and it is still being performed. But the vital
"relevance" of twenty years ago has gone. The political wit
that once had a bitter sharpness or boldness is hardly
understood today. In those days the reference to Himmler
could still cause a shudder, for Himmler's rule with the
guillotine was only just over. It is much the same today,
however, as if making sport of the Swiss Chaudet. But
enough of that. For me it was a healthy cold shower. It
strengthened me in the opinion that now, precisely now,
I should come back to the same material *in a very different
way*, looking at the ideas and hopes and antitheses, and
especially the example and legacy of those who gave their
lives at that time. This is a hard task and I can only begin
with a trial run. So help me God, as the Americans say.

The cold shower reminds me that I, too,[3] sprinkle myself twice each day with the cold water of Saas, in both
summer and winter. I hope I shall still be able to do so at
your age. The urological examination at Zurich turned out

well. No surgery need be performed at the moment; the functioning is satisfactory. The internist told me that if I would give up drinking and smoking, my blood pressure and circulation would improve. But I thought I should then be *too* healthy, and that seems to be dangerous in old age. One then dies of a stroke. So I will continue to live as usual so long as I can work and walk.

The main thing is that you should have good news of your wife and that she should come back cured from the mountains. My own wife sends sincere greetings to you both.

Thanks again for your hospitality and for the good words in your note,

With all good wishes,

Yours,
CARL ZUCKMAYER

---

[1]For the circular letter cf. *Briefe 1961–68*, pp. 475–480; ET *Letters*, pp. 295–298 (No. 287). It was a Roman Catholic priest who called Barth "the church father of the Bruderholz" (quoted in this letter).

[2]Barth refers to this garden (our "Gertli") in the above letter.

[3]Barth refers to his summer and winter cold showers in the above letter.

Dear Friend,

The month of June is nearly over, and before this happens I want to have answered your fine letter of the 5th.

It was truly a joy for me that in spite of everything you were able to visit our house—which is not remotely to be compared with your home in the Saas-Fee mountains—and that you have good recollections of the few close friends that I invited to meet you. Your visit is still recalled here with particular pleasure. When you say that Mrs. Busch-Blum is a sight for sore eyes I agree with you— apart from her many other qualities. This description will cling to her, coming from a connoisseur like yourself.

I am also very pleased that the Zurich doctors gave you a good report. As regards their admonitions, I am of the same mind as yourself; a little of what we fancy—in the complex relation of soul and body—does us good. But in enjoying the good gifts of God, remember that we want to see you for a long time yet in "the land of the living," as the Old Testament puts it.[1]

It is a comfort to me that you, too, were not very happy about the Basel performance of *Des Teufels General* because, as you see it, the situation of 1933–1945 is no longer our own situation and the burning problems of that time are no longer our problems. The impact of the *Seelenbräu*,[2] which, if I am right, you wrote from the heart as an American emigrant, as you also wrote the *General*, will in my view be more lasting than the more relevant *General* because the material, for all its local setting, expresses and addresses something timeless.

This brings me to the anxiety I have already expressed about the new work you are undertaking. I have no doubt that as a product of your open, profound, and cheerful spirit this will be in its way a great and beautiful thing. But the subject matter, the subject matter? I am simply afraid that

the conspiracy that failed in 1944, even in the very inter-
esting interpretation and presentation that you will undoubtedly give it, will not be able to have more than an
artistic impact on the eyes and ears of the present generation, for all their respect for your ability and achievement.
Whose enthusiasm can you kindle for the inner problems
of the Kreisauer Circle[3] when the thoughts of the best of
people center at best on Vietnam, Paris, Biafra, or Bonn
(the emergency regulations)? It may have had, within certain limits, a very remarkable past—but do you seriously
think that it has a future and thus deserves to be set on a
candlestick again as a light for our path? I still remember
as if it were yesterday how what Dietrich Bonhoeffer told
me personally about the venture, or the conversations pre-
ceding it, gave me the impression of something hopelessly
passé. And when, in 1945, the only survivor of 1944, the
present President of the Republic, whom I cannot regard
as a good man, made out that he was a prophet of the
matter, for all my human sympathy for the fate of the
participants, it seemed to me that it was truly a dead end
which did not offer the light of any promise for the future.
Until I am better instructed, of course! Perhaps the work
you are now taking in hand will bring this better instruc-
tion to me and others of our age. A book I am now reading,
O.-E. Schüddekopf's *Linke Leute von rechts* (Kohlham-
mer, 1960), might be of interest to you because of the way
in which it sets the episode in its broader historical context. But perhaps you know it already.

Things are going well here. After five weeks in Adelboden my wife came back refreshed and strengthened. My
problem is just to see that she gets the rest she needs and
to protect her from all physical work—which is by no
means easy. I myself can manage my little labors as an
emeritus relatively calmly and satisfactorily. This spring
and summer—apart from my ecumenical endeavors, of
which I recently sent a sample in *Orientierung*[4]—Schleiermacher has dominated the scene. You will be receiving,
when it is ready, a selection from his works (not prepared
by me) with a longer epilogue by me,[5] a rather autobio-

graphically tinged survey of my own relations with this man who was born 200 years ago. Have you read, or heard on the radio, that the Academy for Poetry and Speech has awarded me a Sigmund Freud prize; what has been found prize-worthy is my "academic prose." To receive this prize I shall be going to Darmstadt (if I am still alive) with my wife and doctor at the end of October, and then we shall naturally go to Mainz to see our relatives and definitely to visit the cathedral in which, according to your story,[6] such a terrible thing took place.

Have you any plausible explanation for the fact that my "Thanks and Greetings,"[7] which is known to you, was read by my wife and various more distant friends with the same pleasure with which I wrote it, but has not been well received by the other members of my immediate family? Perhaps because they know me only too well?!

Last Monday I had to endure a seven-headed television team for four hours. But you know this game as well as I do from long experience. *O tempora, O mores!*

Enough of this chatter. With true and sincere greetings and asking you to remember me kindly to your wife,

Yours,
KARL BARTH

[1]Ps. 27:13; 116:9; Isa. 28:11; 53:8, etc.

[2]The story "Der Seelenbräu" was published in Zuckmayer's *Meistererzählungen* (Frankfurt, 1967), pp. 119–189.

[3]The Kreisauer Circle, led by Helmuth James von Moltke, took part in the conspiracy that led to the attempt on Hitler's life on July 20, 1944.

[4]Cf. the interview with Barth published as "Am Runden Tisch. Evangelischer Professor und katholische Vikare zur Sache der Verkündigung," in *Orientierung. Katholische Blätter für weltanschauliche Information*, 32, No. 11 (Zurich, June 15, 1968), pp. 134f.

[5]*Schleiermacher-Auswahl. Mit einem Nachwort von Karl Barth* (Munich/Hamburg, 1968).

[6]For the story "Die Fastnachtsbeichte" (1959) cf. *Meistererzählungen* (Frankfurt, 1967), pp. 355–476.

[7]Barth's Circular Letter (see n. 1, p. 51).

Saas-Fee, August 6, 1968

Dear Friend,

Sincere thanks for dedicating the Schleiermacher and your epilogue to me. I am eager to read it and am keeping the autumn for it; at the moment we are swarming with visitors. I hope you and your wife are in the best of health and greet you both with all good wishes,

Yours,
CARL ZUCKMAYER

Dear Friend,

I am a little worried that since my last letter of June 29 all I have heard from you is a friendly card. I hope this is not connected with any deterioration of your health, which, like my own, is none too stable. And how much worse if my last letter caused you some displeasure at the point where I thought I should express my doubts about your latest large project. I can very well imagine that a thinker and poet like yourself might not take too kindly to it if, when he is pregnant with a definite idea, a third person casts doubt on it, as I did, before it comes to birth. Who am I to advise you in your own field in which I have no expertise? If, then, your long silence is related to this passage in my letter, I will close my mouth—*si tacuissem, philosophus mansissem*—and say no more about the matter, but simply assure you that whatever you have written or may still write moves and concerns me almost "as if it were a part of me."

My own life these past months has been unduly but unavoidably controlled by events in the less honorable members of my body. My friend Dr. Briellmann in fact saved my life by diagnosing a dangerous bowel development with threatened ruptures, being proved right by an immediate operation (the same night the Russians marched into Czechoslovakia!).[1] The doctors at the city hospital did wonders in their own way and checked the disorder, as they said, for another thirty (!) years. During the hours after the surgery, according to the night nurse looking after me, I gave incessant expression to some lofty but to her unintelligible ecumenical and other theology. Supposing I had on this occasion related some old and new love stories from my long life! There then followed sixteen days in hospital with intravenous feeding, thirst (I now know for the first time what thirst is!), and lots of penicillin injections. But I am now over it all and for the moment, truly weary, am facing the question whether our Father in heaven is indicating to me by all this either that I should keep quiet and leave the talking to the younger generation, or, conversely, that another period of grace has been granted me which I should use to complete some secondary tasks at my desk as best I can (as I attempted in my Schleiermacher epilogue this summer).

What are your thoughts about the present student unrest throughout the world? And the Soviet move to the immediate East? And Biafra? And the encyclical on the pill[2] issued by the undoubtedly well-meaning but neither very wise nor energetic Paul VI (to whom I have to write a letter, although on another matter)?[3] And what seems to be threatening on the Suez Canal (roughly where Pharaoh was drowned and Miriam sang her victory song)?[4] May it be that once again we must postulate the imminent coming again of the Lord (*unde iterum venturus est*)? Eberhard Busch (the fortunate husband of Mrs. Sight for Sore Eyes) is at work on a theological masterpiece on an eighteenth-century man[5] who, in addition to other and more important things, became famous because on the basis of acute deliberations he thought he could prophesy the coming of this much to be desired event exactly in the year 1836. What actually happened that year was the appearance of the *Life of Jesus* of David Friedrich Strauss, who no less acutely believed he could prove that this life is in fact known only in a garland of myths!

Practical questions facing me are: 1) whether I can hold my winter colloquium (this time on predestination for and against Calvin), and 2) whether the trip to Darmstadt and Mainz at the end of October will be feasible. God will provide.[6]

With sincere greetings (to you and all yours),

Yours,
KARL BARTH

---

[1]August 21/22, 1968.
[2]The encyclical of Paul VI, "Humanae vitae," July 25, 1968.
[3]For Barth's letter to Paul VI, Sept. 28, 1968, see *Briefe 1961–68*, pp. 499–502; ET *Letters*, pp. 312–14 (No. 303).
[4]Miriam's victory song may be found in Exod. 15:20f.
[5]Johann Albrecht Bengel, 1687–1752.
[6]See Gen. 22:8.

Saas-Fee, September 26, 1968

Dear Friend,

To my concern I learned today through Prof. Geiger that you have had surgery and have been in hospital. I will not tire you with a long letter but simply say how much I hope and pray for your recovery. Perhaps you are already in that state of convalescence which I have always found to be particularly beautiful, contemplative, and rich in thinking after a severe illness and an operation.

Hoping that all goes well with you and your dear wife, with sincere wishes and greetings from both of us,

Yours,
CARL ZUCKMAYER

Dear Friend,

Please, for God's sake, do not think that the passage in your last long letter, in which you were so kind as to discuss my latest project (sketched for you in conversation) and to express doubts about it, either did or could cause me any displeasure. I see in it only friendly sharing in my work, for which I am grateful. I am not one of those people who can tolerate only agreement, but am grateful for criticism when it is kindly disposed. My long silence is due to the fact that I am terribly burdened with this work and constantly have to overcome doubts and difficulties—both inner and technical—and to steer around cliffs—yet I cannot break away from it, although often I am not certain whether I have not undertaken something impossible and will one day have to put it away in a chest as an unfinished work. During the summer I was almost tempted to abandon the whole thing and give myself up again—finally—to simple cheerfulness, but then came the political crisis in the East and the resultant confusion in our own circles, and I found it necessary to attempt a clarification of possible foundations (for a human society, for a concept of the "freedom of the Christian" who is a "servant of all," according to Luther). Now in the golden clarity of October days I believe I see light and am swimming again with the current. So help me God, as the Americans say. They have a habit of saying this without thinking about it, but I truly think that if God truly wills it, I can succeed in conjuring a spark of humor and glimmer of cheerfulness even out of this stern and bitter stuff. I have twenty-three pages of dialogue all ready like rows of notes or chords; they have still to be put in sentences or harmonized. The task now is one of composition.

My health is good; a certain instability does not alter

this much. I have had an unsettled summer: many visits, and not all of them as welcome as yours last year. My memoirs have brought not only beautiful and valuable new friendships, like yours or the link with Emil Staiger, but also a swarm of inquisitive people and so-called admirers—both male and especially female—who unfortunately are not always a sight for sore eyes but force me into prattle rather than conversation, and since one cannot always shake them off they cost a great deal of time and energy. This has also kept me back from letter writing. So long as it is high season here, there are people in front of the house almost every day trying at least to catch me or photograph me on my walk. This is in part well meant, but is very wearing. Now in the autumn things are different; I am alone here with my wife and can concentrate on my work. An unexpected visit was very stimulating and enjoyable; Dr. Hermann Volk, the bishop of my native town of Mainz, came to see me—perhaps you know his theological writings. He is a man of great knowledge and wide intellectual horizons. He read Sunday mass here a couple of times and boldly climbed the Allalin with me, even though it was covered with new snow. If you can manage your trip to Mainz, you will perhaps meet him and will probably get on well with him. But perhaps you should put off such a strenuous undertaking after your severe operation. Yet I believe that the hint from above which a severe illness and especially your almost miraculous survival and recovery undoubtedly signifies will give you courage above all to remain at work, and I very much hope that the pipe smoke is already curling again at the desk in the quiet study on the Bruderholz, and that the excellent Dr. Briellmann often opens a bottle again!

With fondest and sincerest greetings and good wishes to you and your wife, from my wife too,

Yours,
CARL ZUCKMAYER

More about other things when time permits.

Dear Herr Busch,

I must beg your pardon, indeed, I am ashamed, that I have not thanked you long since for your valuable account (of July 18)[1] and the enclosed writings, your memorial address and the *Final Testimonies*.[2] I have often done so in thought and as a weak excuse can only plead that in July I was overburdened with correspondence, unavoidable tasks, and visits, that in August I went on a long trip that took me to such geographically distant places as the South Tyrol and Stockholm, and that when we came back home at the end of September to a perfect autumn in the high mountains—as always at this time of the year and after a journey all the dams and sluices burst open—it was only then that I could finally get down to the productive work whose temporary drying up—a long ebb—was connected in a remarkable way with the death of Karl Barth.

The assumption in your letter of July 18 is wrong; I remember you very well, and by no means only as the fortunate husband of Mrs. Sight for Sore Eyes (whom Karl Barth mentioned by this name in his last letter to me). I also knew you as someone who had been published, for he had previously sent me your work *Humane Theologie*,[3] which I read with great interest. And I even knew that you were born in Witten in 1937. Please, then, accept my belated thanks as sincere and as those of a friend, even though our acquaintance is slight.

What you told me about the last days and the peaceful homegoing of our great and respected friend was a gift and a great comfort to me. I had had no other details and had often wondered how it had happened, whether he was cut down by death, resisting and struggling to the last death-rattle—which was quite conceivable in view of his defiant vitality—or whether he was taken with a gentle hand. Yes,

I think one can speak of a grace in death—which a great poet once called "the mildest form of life, the masterpiece of eternal love."[4] The consoling picture of his hands still folded for evening prayer is constantly with me. In one who may die thus is the love that does not count the cost but is stronger than the most righteous wrath. I received only kindness and warmth from him, and the stringent and postulating way in which he conducted dialogue always benefited and strengthened me—although I was shocked, and felt a new kind of responsibility, when in one of his very first letters to me he told me that in my obviously purely "secular" work I was discharging, and had to discharge, a priestly office. This struck "holy terror" into me at the time, but I also found how beneficial and necessary this is—at a time of life and after experiences which mean that the "world" is hardly able to shock one any more. But terror is just as indispensable as wonder— if one is not to be speechless before the world and its Creator.

Seldom has the news of someone's death hit me so hard—it came most unexpectedly after he had survived his last operation—and had such an effect on my own life. On the evening when we met in the Bruderholz, I spent a couple of hours alone with him and told him about my new dramatic project—which he did not like. It would take us too far afield in a letter to explain this, but his arguments were convincing, and in particular they fed doubts about the matter that I already had. Nevertheless, I advanced counterarguments and would not give up the project. In conclusion he said: "But if you *must*—then attempt it! I would be glad to be wrong." I did attempt it, but always with the reservation or proviso that as soon as it had taken on a recognizable form, I would go to Basel and he should say Yes or No. But there was no time for this. His death told me: No. I gave up the plan and was lying fallow. I now believe: For the best.

Your burial address moved me greatly—and I am glad to have a copy of *Final Testimonies*. How beautiful that his last, incomplete work has the title: "Starting Out, Turning Round, Confessing."[5]

I had another reason for the long delay in writing to you. For I wanted to send on a work on which I have been engaged since his death. It is to be called "Story of a Late Friendship," and I would have liked to publish it in the memorial edition of the *Neue Zürcher Zeitung* last spring. But I am a slow worker with material that affects me personally, and this needed distance and time to mature. I hope to be able to finish and publish it by December 10 this year.

Sincere greetings to yourself and your dear wife, and wishing you the health and strong cheerfulness of soul that radiated so wonderfully from the old pipe-smoker in the Bruderholz,

Yours,
CARL ZUCKMAYER

[1]E. Busch had sent Zuckmayer a letter telling him about Barth's last days and the circumstances of his death on December 10, 1968.

[2]For Busch's eulogy at Barth's burial in the Basel cemetery see *Karl Barth 1886–1968. Gedenkfeier im Basler Münster* (Zurich, 1969), pp. 13–19; for Busch's letter see the second edition of Barth's *Letzte Zeugnisse* (Zurich, 1969), with an epilogue by Busch.

[3]E. Busch, *Humane Theologie. Texte und Erläuterungen zur Theologie des alten Karl Barth* (Zurich, 1967).

[4]Gerhart Hauptmann, *Michael Kramer* (1900), end of Act IV.

[5]This fragment may be found in *Letzte Zeugnisse*, pp. 61–71; ET *Final Testimonies* (Grand Rapids, 1977), pp. 53–60). Barth was at work on it the evening before his death.

STORY OF A LATE FRIENDSHIP
In Memory of Karl Barth

As often happens, particularly on very special occasions, this encounter began by being within a hair's breadth of never taking place at all. In the spring of 1967 I had been on a long trip to Italy, partly to escape my mail. Six months after the publication of my memoirs the flood had swollen to such proportions that my wife and I almost collapsed at the daily approach of the mailman. "Do not send on any letters," was the motto of this journey, which was meant also to give me time to consider whether my book was really so bad as to trigger such an explosion of readers. At home a regulatory hand sorted out the daily yield, my assumption being that it would know how to separate the wheat from the chaff. This nearly proved fatal. But accidentally or otherwise, on my return a thick bundle fell to the floor on which this hand had inscribed: "Other letters from unknown people to be answered briefly." On lifting it up I found *this* letter, and stared unbelievingly at the name of the sender. Could it be that this "unknown person" was really Karl Barth?

"Someone has given me a copy of your book *Als wär's ein Stück von mir*," this letter began. "I read it at a sitting. And now I am forced to say. . . ." What he said was not the usual stuff. It was an appeal that came home to me and affected me as few others have ever done.

"First of all, I simply enjoyed your style," and he then showed how and why the reading pleased him. There was something remarkable about this exposition—not only in understanding and warmth, but also in an almost childlike and unconcealed wonder. It was as if somebody had visited a zoo for the first time. "Much more than you, I am a child of the nineteenth century; and the modern world of letters, the theater, the cinema, and—how shall I put it—noble Bohemianism, has certainly affected me but never grasped or touched me closely. . . ."

But then came the most astounding thing of all; he found it necessary to say: "I am an Evangelical theologian," and there followed a brief synopsis of his career with a stress in the main on its beginning, when he was a real pastor in Geneva and the Aargau. "I have written many stout and slim volumes of practical, historical, and above all—do not be alarmed!—dogmatic theology." He closed by saying: "I now live in quiet but busy retirement. I value the presence of loving women, good wine, and a constantly burning pipe. . . . I say all this so as to tell you something about who is writing and who it is that takes such pleasure in thinking about you."

Enclosed with his letter were two works, the story of his visit to Rome with reflections on it, *Ad limina Apostolorum*, and a collection of his four addresses on Mozart. The latter was already known to me. The former, with a letter on mariology as an appendix, soon provided material for discussion and disagreement between us. For the most beautiful thing for me in our rich oral and written discussions was this, that notwithstanding a deep, basic agreement, there were always things about which we differed. He could then in a frank exchange spark his opposite number with a dark, fiery glance like a burning coal, half stern, half amused, and at the same time full of sympathy and joy.

After the first exchange of letters, which took place in June 1967, our first meeting took place soon after in July. At his express wish it did so at my home here in Saas-Fee. He was then staying, perhaps for the last time, as he said rather ominously, here in the Valais mountains in the summer residence of his son Markus Barth in the Val d'Hérens. As the younger—he was 81 and I only 70—I naturally offered to visit him there. But he would not have this—he insisted, as he wrote, that he wanted to get to know me "in my own skin." "We are perfectly natural only in our own home." He himself was natural wherever he was. Nor was he scared off by the fact that one cannot get here by car, but it is necessary to climb up for fifteen to twenty minutes from the station and parking-place at Saas-Fee. As it was, I brought an electric car, used only to carry freight, so that he could ride a good stretch of the way. On the return journey, however, after several hours of talk and many a good drop, he went on foot, supported only on the arm of his wife and vigorously refusing any other aid.

It was a glorious day. The glaciers and snowy summits shone upon him. But his main interest was in people. At the aperitif, on our shady terrace, he gathered me up in prayer and asked Gretchen's question:[1] "How about you and religion? I mean, Roman Catholicism? Is it a romantic memory—or does it mean something to you?" At first this embarrassed me. A complex question, and we were sitting there as two families, four Barths and four Zuckmayers. Noting this, he said: "We will talk about this later in private," and then he looked imperiously at my wife and said: "After eating, you must leave us two old men alone." Seldom have I met so young a spirit as in the conversation that followed. And after long and candid exchanges he suddenly gave me the completely unhoped for surprise of personal confidence—to someone he was seeing for the first time.

This talk lasted two and a half hours, and I had the remarkable impression that I myself was the older in attitude—very watchful, suspicious, and tentative on alien territory—while he was wholly in his element, inspired, stormy, and daring. Naturally we talked about literature, the arts, and especially music. Here he manifested a certain impatience, almost onesidedness. Mozart, about whom few, and not even Annette Kolb, have written finer things than he has, was for him the absolute summit of attainable perfection, all else being either ascent to him or descent from him. He often said—and even wrote—that he believed that when the angels had time off from singing Alleluias and could make music for their own pleasure they would sing only Mozart (whom he humorously commended to the pope for beatification). I ventured to suggest that they might sometimes turn to Schubert for a change. But this did not suit him; Schubert was too Romantic, and Romanticism was suspect for him, in philosophy as well. Beethoven came off worst of all—with the "desperate jubilation" (or what he later called "unredeemed shout of joy") of the last movement of his Ninth Symphony. Again, the Missa Solemnis did not seem to him to come from a liberated heart but from a tortured mind. As regards the end of the Ninth Symphony, I agreed with him, but I pointed to the "other Beethoven" of the last piano sonatas like Opus 111, and the late chamber music like the wonderful string quartet Opus 135, with its third movement, the lento assai. "Yes, I know," he said impatiently. "They call this metaphysical music. That is just what it is. In Beethoven everything has to mean something. When people sing a theme from Beethoven, they pull solemn faces. But then," he suddenly said with that odd spark of laughter in his eyes, "I am not the least bit musical," and after some variations on this he broke off the subject. It was a lively and moving afternoon: midsummer, and the air full of the scent of hay through the open window. During the last half-hour of the conversation he frequently laid his hand on mine and softly said things that were not meant for anyone else—I answered as best I could, and even if both of us had been much younger this ending to a serious but cheerful antiphon would have initiated an exchange that could never end.

After this visit, and until my own visit to Basel the following year, and beyond that, there followed a lively correspondence which became increasingly intimate and was not without some thrusts and counter-thrusts. The address "Dear and Honored," or "Dear Herr," soon gave way on his part to a simple "Dear Friend." But in his very first letter after that day in July, one dated August 15, 1967, he startled me. He had read in the meantime almost everything I had published, and he decided in favor of the volume of stories as the work that had made the deepest impression on him (much to my pleasure, for I regard it as superior to my better-known works). But then came the shock. What moved him, he wrote, what gave the advantage to this book over the products of other contemporaries, whom he named, was to be found "in the never-failing compassion with which it is constantly given you to view human darkness, corruption, and misery. Mephistopheles is absent. . . . And the best is that you yourself hardly notice how much in what one might call your purely 'secular' writings you have in fact discharged, and still discharge, a priestly office, and do so to a degree that is granted to few professional priests, preachers, and theologians, either Roman or Evangelical." This smote me to the ground more than any harsh expert criticism ever could have done. I felt hit by a claim or postulate one can harldy meet *consciously*. Happily one forgets this when at work. The absence of Mephistopheles also troubled me at first, for critics, even friends, and I myself, had often seen this as a defect. These statements struck me and pulled me up short, but the effect was totally transformed by the overflowing kindness and refreshing sympathy of his letters. At the end of his letter he wrote: "I greet you as a friend, or rather as a younger brother, whom I found only late but with all the greater gratitude."

Naturally I myself had tried to become better acquainted with his theological work, to the extent that "lay people" (he could not stand the term) can do so. He sent me Volume II,2 of his *Dogmatics*, since in our talk we had touched on the difficult theme of predestination. This and the figure and work of Calvin provided material for much dialogue and even debate. He sent me the noble and spirited sermons that he had preached in the Basel prison (*Deliverance to the Captives*), in which, as he wrote, he had tried to present such problems in a simple way to the simple man, "or not so simple in this case."

His thirst for knowledge, fed from a spring of deep

basic knowledge, was inexhaustible, and increased my own. He constantly took up new themes of a historical, literary, or philosophical character, in order, as he put it, to fill long-standing gaps. Thus he had suddenly lighted on Wilhelm Raabe and at the same time on Jean-Paul Sartre (*Les Mots*). "Both have touched me," he wrote, "but in a rather *sinister* way" (his own underlining). "Raabe with the primitive German amiability of his depictions seems to me to be one of the refined representatives of the secret nihilism of the nineteenth century, while Sartre with his hardly incidental ice-cold sharpness in relation to himself seems to be the crude representative of the open nihilism of the present century." These and similar questions were really meant as questions and not as assertions. He accepted contradiction and often demanded it, dealing with it humorously; and how remarkable and inspiring was this play, the play of thoughts, of questions and answers, often reminding me of Nicolaus Cusanus, in its effect on the intellectual vitality of one who is aging but by no means finished with himself. Then Schleiermacher became the subject of discussion. Apart from his relation to the Romantics, the *Briefe über Lucinde*, and the *Reden über die Religion*, I knew very little about him, and it was only through my new friend, and his comprehensive epilogue to a new selection, that I came to know more. Writing about a new, critical seminar, Barth said: "For the moment I am enjoying it (with the old love/hate and the even older hate/love)." In every letter during his "busy retirement," he had to report some new plans and projects and controversies. Could he manage a lectures series which he had been invited to give in America at Harvard University? Should he begin a seminar for and against Calvin? "In a salutary way this has made me put in a good deal of work, but it has also given me much pleasure, both on account of the material and also because I greatly enjoy dealing and speaking with the (some) 60 young people. . . ." "Do you know the pretty little story about Pablo Casals?" the same letter asks. "He is now 90 years old—so much older than either of us—and he still practices four to five hours every day. When asked why, he answered: 'Because I have the impression I am making progress.' "

Everything concerning everyday life and world events and daily politics occupied him and aroused his criticism and lively interest, for example, the then coalition government in Bonn, which he viewed very sharply, quite apart from the fact that "a supposedly 'Christian' party is in principle an abomination to me, especially when it is in power," or the "turmoil of the Confederate elections" in the autumn of 1967: "The Valais Socialist Dellberg, who is my age and no longer endorsed by his own party, ran magnificently on his own and was convincingly re-elected." He also told the story of an immature theological student from Canada who had just come to him that morning and asked what reason meant for his theology. "Answer: I use it!"

Never has any person in our day, with the possible exception of Albert Einstein, so convinced me by his mere existence that faith in God is rational.

The time came for my visit to his home in the Bruderholz in Basel, which he had long desired. For me this was the highpoint in this late friendship, and I had no sense or premonition of parting. I saw his "little manse garden," which he loved, in all its May glory. We sat alone in the afternoon and with a few close friends in the evening, surrounded by the smoke of his pipe in his cosy study, where, between walls covered with bookshelves, he worked like Jerome in his cage. But he was particularly proud of his "modern desk." The friends were much younger—his last assistant Eberhard Busch and his charming wife, whom to his merriment I called a sight for sore eyes, and his excellent physician Dr. Briellmann, who generously opened bottles of red wine, knowing that this would not hurt him but simply stimulate him and enliven our gathering. He was frail, more so than when I first knew him, his health weakened by severe operations, but so far as possible he disregarded this. His intellectual fire and

71

cheerful sympathy for the active, healthy life were stronger than sickness and the burden of age. "Brother body," as he jocularly called it, caused him a great deal of trouble in his last year, his 83rd. But immediately after a stay in hospital with serious surgery, intravenous feeding, and thirst—"I now know for the first time what thirst is!" he wrote—he was full of new energy and projects and took a lively interest in my own plans. That the German Academy for Speech and Poetry awarded him the Sigmund Freud prize for "academic prose" amused him greatly, but I had the impression that, having received few public honors, he was greatly pleased by it. He died on December 10, 1968 after a full day of reading and conversation, and according to all accounts I believe that he died a very peaceful death.

In his last circular letter of "Thanks and Greetings" after his 82nd birthday he made a beautiful reference to me and to our "remarkable friendship" and "lively correspondence." But I myself had found once again what all of us most need if we are to know ourselves: a father figure.

CARL ZUCKMAYER

[1]This question, which Gretchen puts to Faust in Goethe's tragedy, is "Do you believe in God?"

832.912
B284

66733

DEMCO 38-297   Lincoln Christian College